WHO INVENTED RAIN?

Bil Keane

FAWCETT GOLD MEDAL • NEW YORK

A Fawcett Gold Medal Book
Published by Ballantine Books
Copyright © 1981, 1986 by Cowles Syndicate, Inc.

Library of Congress Catalog Card Number: 86-90875

ISBN 0-449-12423-1

Manufactured in the United States of America

First Ballantine Books Edition: June 1986

10 9 8 7 6 5 4 3

"Mommy! It rained worms!"

"The phone's ringing, the front doorbell's
chiming, the dryer's buzzing and the
oven's dinging!"

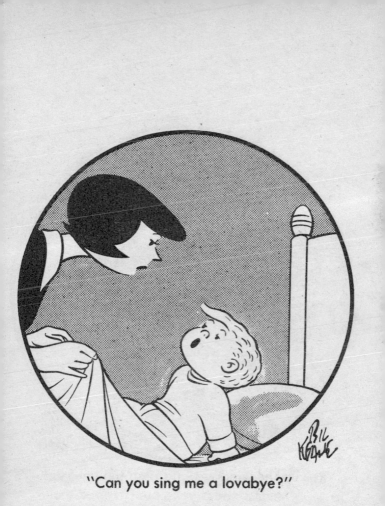

"Can you sing me a lovabye?"

"Roll up the windows and keep the smell in."

"They forgot to put the lid on your sandwich."

"There must be a ballgame over there."

"I hafta watch 'General Hospital' for Grandma
while she's on the phone."

"There's something wrong with this ball. The one's on TV go over the net lots more."

"I don't like kissing Daddy on Saturdays 'cause his whiskers hurt my face."

"Grandma uses the bottom part for reading,
the top part for looking out the window,
and the middle for watching TV."

"If they lived happily ever after, does that mean they're still alive?"

"I'm just tying up all the loose ends."

"He's playing with me now. You can't have him."

"Barfy's tasting PJ!"

"Is this when God said 'Let there be cars'?"

"Mommy! Jeffy's going to eat off one of your collector's plates!"

"It's a very GOOD elephant, Jeffy. Daddy was stupid to think it was a doggy."

"Yeah? Well, MY father's flown on a 707, a 727, a 747 AND a DC 10!"

"Do you have anything rated G?"

"Jeffy isn't even waiting till it's planted."

"The Powells have one of those microwave cameras that make the pictures right away."

"When I grow taller than Mommy I'm going to marry her."

"Don't worry about having seconds. It's decaffeinated."

"Barfy's being a naughty doggy, Mommy! He's settin' foot in the street!"

"That man said an X-rated word."

"This is the upper deck."

"Grandma's really smart. She said, 'Hi, Dolly'
before I told her who I was."

"Wanna try something new, Mommy? It's a potato chip sandwich."

"Is it easier now, Daddy? I moved the stick to
'P' for 'Push!'"

"Grandma won't let go of the dollar till you say,
'Thank you.'"

"Aw, Mommy, not a shower! Please?"

"Jeffy! It's the Goodyear rocket."

"PJ's touching the map ball."

"My bike did something dumb."

"I like broccoli OK. My taste bugs don't like it."

"A good night's sleep makes you grow."

"How much bigger did I get last night, Mommy?"

"A million, a billion, a trillion . . . what comes
after a trillion?"

"A trillion and one."

"I pledge deletions to the flag . . . ."

"Will you come here and blow my nose for me, Mommy?"

"It's a new game, Mommy. Want me to tell you
how to play it?"

"Couldn't you bring my lunch out here, Mommy?"

"Steve's stepmother isn't wicked. She gave us cookies."

"Ketchup? Mustard?"

"Just leave mine blank."

"She's playin' a tangerine."

"We made our own lunch to save you work."

"You don't have to hug me this time, Mommy.
We won!"

"I can't remember, Mommy. Which little piggy is which?"

"If I keep my lightening bugs in my room I won't need a night light, and that'll save energy."

"They must be growing up. They don't need pushes any more."

"Did you know you can't toast marshmallows in a toaster?"

"We're s'posed to forgive and forget. Well, I forgive Jeffy for eating my candy bar, but I'll never forget it."

"The water's too warm."

"Jeffy! Turn around here and mind your own business."

"I can't stop my tongue from goin' in the hole where my tooth was."

"Look, Mommy! I can swim!"

"Water!"

"She's comforting him, not burping him."

"This is a mommy stringbean! It has little baby beans inside."

"I don't want the water hot or cold. I want it middle."

"We don't know WHAT we're makin' yet. We just started."

"Whose armrest is this, Mommy? Mine or Billy's?"

"Diddle, diddle, dumpling, mice and John. . . ."

"Look, I've bitten out Idaho!"

"Dolly isn't playin' fair! She says she's bulletproof!"

"Jeffy, you're not giving your goldfish too much food, are you?"

"No, Mommy."

"What time is when the big hand is on five and the little hand is on the floor?"

"Why does that boat have curtains on it?"

"Billy digs the peanuts out and leaves potholes in the brittle."

"How many choices do we get for dinner
tonight, Mommy?"

"Two: Take it or leave it."

"Why do some grandmas have blue hair?"

"The sink won't swallow."

"Whenever I'm in those weeds it starts raining
in my eyes."

"Oh, boy! Pie a la king!"

"I stubbed my belbow!"

"Mommy, this button keeps getting out."

"You just wait till the designated hitter gets home."

"I didn't MEAN to hit him. My hand slipped."

"Can we see your virus, Mommy?"

"The telephone man's here and he's a girl!"

"That's my ball, Jeffy. Don't use up all the bounces."

"Don't clap, Mommy. If he thinks you're
applaudin' he'll never stop."

"Come on, take it. It won't bite you."

"Daddy doesn't need a life jacket 'cause the
captain has to go down with the ship."

"Your plant in the bottle looked thirsty, Mommy, so I gave it a good drink."

"Turn on 'Sesame Street' Grandma, so we can learn our numbers."

"Mommy says dinner will be ready in 20
minutes if I help her, 10 minutes if I don't."

"If I was borned in the hospital, who came to
buy me and bring me home?"

"My dad says someday I'll LIKE kissing girls,
but so far I only like pulling their hair."

"Now we can practice for the beach!"

"Slow down, Daddy. I want to see the corn."

"Can you unpack our bathing suits and take us
down on the beach, Mommy?"

"Know what, Mommy? They gift-wrapped the toilet seat!"

"My eyes are too sunny."

"Open it up and let the shade out, Daddy."

"Is the water warm enough for us to go in, Daddy?"

"Don't go out too far, Jeffy! You're not s'posed
to cross the ocean alone!"

"Daddy, how much is it a wave?"

"I taste like a peanut!"

"It's Billy and Jeffy's fault. They were doing
their Indian rain dance."

"The lady at the office says this is 'zactly what
they need 'cause it's been so dry."

"On this card to Grandma do I hafta say
'havin' a good time?'"

"The rain stopped, sun's out! Isn't anybody
interested in going to the beach?"

"Will you put this in your pocket, Mommy?"

"I can hear the ocean better if I DON'T put the
shell to my ear."

"Gulls are lucky. They stay at the seashore all year."

"Look, Daddy! Those people sure have
a lot of pets!"

"Home again, home again, jiggety j . . .
. . . oops! NOW I remember what I didn't do
before we left."

"Now I know why they call this Labor Day.
Gettin' ready to go back to school
is real LABOR."

"I'm not too happy about the start of
school either."

"I need a new football. I don't know if I should
send up a prayer, write a letter to Santa Claus
or call grandma."

"Mommy! Somebody put a B on your sign
during the night!"

"All the kids in my class are comin' to our garage sale. They don't have any money, but they like to watch."

"Here comes a customer, Mommy! Are we open
for business?"

" . . . then my mommy said to daddy, 'We'll
get rid of all the junk around this place.' "

"This is a neat party we're havin', Mommy! Is everybody staying for lunch?"

"Mommy! Jeffy and PJ keep bringing out the clothes from your bedroom closet!"

"Mommy! Daddy just sold the $10 pole lamp to that lady for $5!"

"Quick, Dolly! Run in the house and bring me
your piggy bank. I've run out of change."

"Oh boy! We have enough good stuff left to
have another garage sale next week!"

"Why are some of your clubs
wearing mittens?"

"Mommy, will you fix the color on this toaster?"

"I wish God wouldn't wash the world on Saturdays."

"A penny for your thoughts."　"Make it a quarter, Mommy, and we're in business."

"PJ turned over my box of lions and they're all gettin' away."

"Mommy, why does 'in a minute' take so long?"

You can have lots more fun
with
BIL KEANE and
THE FAMILY CIRCUS